Killing the Presidents:
Presidential Assassinations
And Assassination Attempts

Copyright 2013 by Nicholas L. Vulich

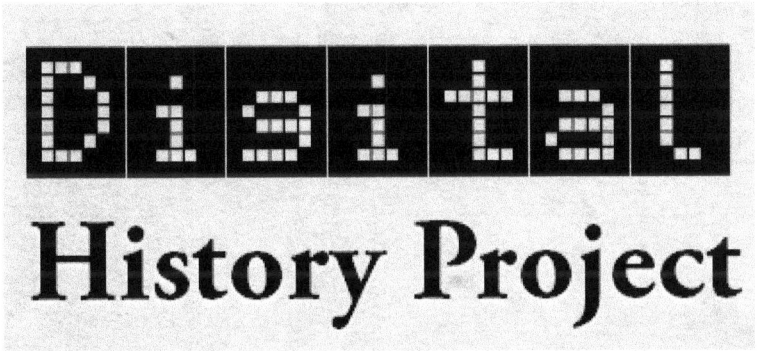

Thank you for purchasing this book. It is designed to give you a brief outline of one aspect of American history. While no book can possibly give you all of the information available relating to the Presidential assassinations, every attempt has been made to bring you all of the important details you need to understand what was happening at the time of each. Our goal is to help you understand historical events by presenting them in easily digestible bites.

If you find the contents helpful, please consider taking a few moments to leave a review on Amazon.

Your comments will help other readers decide if this book may be useful to them in their journey to understand this dark part of American history. They will also help me to catch errors or omissions in this book, and to correct them as quickly as possible.

If you have any comments or questions, feel free to contact me at nick@digitalhistoryproject.com. Any corrections will be addressed in future editions.

Table of Contents

Introduction 5
Abraham Lincoln 7
   Lincoln's Premonitions of His Assassination 9
   Plotting of John Wilkes Booth 11
   Booth Sets His Mind on Assassination 15
   The Fateful Day 17
   Killing President Lincoln 23
   Treachery in the Night 32
   Pursuit and Capture of the Conspirators 35
James Garfield 42
   The President's suffering 46
   Charles J. Guiteau – Assassin 49
   Trial of Charles J. Guiteau 54
William McKinley 59
   The Assassin's statement 66
   The suffering President 69
   Trial and execution of Leon Czolgosz 73
John F. Kennedy 77
   Lee Harvey Oswald 87
   The Warren Commission 90
Presidential Assassination Attempts 93
   Andrew Jackson 93
   Abraham Lincoln 95

Theodore Roosevelt 97
Herbert Hoover 99
Franklin D. Roosevelt 100
Harry Truman 101
Gerald Ford 102
Ronald Reagan 104

Introduction

Assassination of political leaders is nothing exclusive to America.

Shakespeare made a career out of re-telling stories of political intrigue, assassination, and murder. Think Caesar, Hamlet, and Macbeth. Queen Victoria had nearly a dozen attempts made on her life during her sixty some year reign. The assassination of Archduke Francis Ferdinand was one of many factors that helped plunge Europe into World War I.

In America, four presidents have lost their lives to assassin's bullets. Fifteen presidents, besides these, have been victims of assassination attempts, and two others have conspiracy theories circulating regarding their deaths.

This leaves only twenty-two presidents untouched by the assassin's shadow.

This book is going to take a look, first at the presidential assassinations, and the circumstances surrounding them, and second, at some of the various assassination attempts upon our leaders.

In most cases, the assassin is clearly defined. In others, like the assassination of President John F. Kennedy, conspiracy theories abound, but the evidence for them is circumstantial at best. As far back as the assassination of Abraham Lincoln, people have looked for larger conspiracies, rather than examining just the facts. In Lincoln's case, it has been postulated than Secretary of War, Edwin M. Stanton was behind Lincoln's demise. The reasoning was that Stanton did not like Lincoln's lenient policies towards reconstruction of the South.

Mary Todd Lincoln believed that Vice-President Andrew Johnson was behind her husband's death. Many more villains have been identified, including the Roman Catholic Church, a Confederate bid for revenge, or even a group of international bankers.

But, it doesn't end there.

In 1980 Author Clara Rising convinced the family of Zachary Taylor to have his body exhumed to search for evidence of foul play. There was none.

Similar theories are told about the death of Warren G. Harding who died after a week long illness during a tour of Alaska and the Pacific Northwest. The official explanation was that he died due to a heart attack or stroke, but because Mrs. Harding refused to allow an autopsy, conspiracy theories were put forth that she was at fault. See *The Strange Death of President Harding* (1930) by Gaston B. Means.

But, conspiracies are for another tale. This book will tell the facts.

Nicholas L. Vulich
Davenport, Iowa (2013)

Abraham Lincoln

Last picture taken of Abraham Lincoln

March 3rd, 1865, found Abraham Lincoln on horseback, riding towards Petersburg, Virginia, accompanied by his bodyguard William Crook. They were on their way to meet General Ulysses S. Grant, who had just captured Petersburg.

Crook described the grisly scene as they crossed the battlefield, "I can still see one man with a bullet-hole through his forehead and another with both arms shot away." Everywhere around them were strewn dead bodies, and the carnage of war.

The next day, March 4th, Lincoln and Crook started towards Richmond, Virginia with Admiral Porter. Richmond had just fallen, and Porter thought the President should survey the city. Porter felt that Lincoln's appearance there so soon after the fall would help show the South the Government's confidence in her people.

Crook described Richmond as "black with Negroes." Together with Lincoln, and his youngest son Tad, they moved through the streets of Richmond with the Negroes watching in awe, and many of them coming up to shake Lincoln's hand. People stared and watched their every move from behind the safety of their windows. Crook imagined guns being poked through the windows at every turn – pointed at the President.

Nothing happened.

Lincoln returned to the White House on March 9th.

Lincoln's Premonitions of His Assassination

Not much later, on March 14th, Lincoln told Crook,

"Crook, do you know, I believe there are men who want to take my life?" Then after a pause, he said, half to himself, "And I have no doubt they will do it."

At the time Crook and Lincoln were walking past a crowd of drunken rowdies on their way to the War Department to meet with Secretary Stanton.

A similar statement from Lincoln is related by Ward Hill Lamon, Lincoln's biographer and boyhood friend:

> "About ten days ago," said he, "I retired very late. I had been up waiting for important dispatches from the front. I could not have been long in bed when I fell into a slumber, for I was weary. I soon began to dream. There seemed to be a death-like stillness about me. Then I heard subdued sobs, as if a number of people were weeping. I thought I left my bed and wandered downstairs. There the silence was broken by the same pitiful sobbing, but the mourners were invisible. I went from room to room; no living person was in sight, but the same mournful sounds of distress met me as I passed along. I saw light in all the rooms; every object was familiar to me; but where were all the people who

were grieving as if their hearts would break? I was puzzled and alarmed. What could be the meaning of all this? Determined to find the cause of a state of things so mysterious and so shocking, I kept on until I arrived at the East Room, which I entered. There I met with a sickening surprise. Before me was a catafalque, on which rested a corpse wrapped in funeral vestments. Around it were stationed soldiers who were acting as guards; and there was a throng of people, gazing mournfully upon the corpse, whose face was covered, others weeping pitifully. 'Who is dead in the White House?' I demanded of one of the soldiers, 'The President,' was his answer; 'he was killed by an assassin.' Then came a loud burst of grief from the crowd, which woke me from my dream. I slept no more that night; and although it was only a dream, I have been strangely annoyed by it ever since."

"That is horrid!" said Mrs. Lincoln, who was also present. "It is only a dream," responded Mr. Lincoln thoughtfully, it is only a dream, Mary. Let us say no more about it, and try to forget it."

Plotting of John Wilkes Booth

SATAN TEMPTING BOOTH TO THE MURDER OF THE PRESIDENT.

John Wilkes Booth first met Doctor Samuel Mudd in November of 1864 during a trip to Charles County, Maryland, all of the time pretending to be interested in buying some land from him. Over dinner, Booth inquired about the doctor's sentiments, and asked for a letter of introduction to other Southern sympathizers.

Mudd declined to give any information to Booth, becoming suspicious of all his questioning. Mudd determined that Booth had to be a Union spy trying to make him divulge information.

On December 23, 1864, Booth ran into Doctor Mudd again, this time outside of the National Hotel in Washington. Booth was able to convince Mudd to give him an introduction to John Surratt.

Surratt joined the group of conspirators, and because he was the only one of them who lived permanently in Washington, the conspirators met frequently at Mary Surratt's boarding house there. In these meetings Mary Surratt knew Booth as "Pet." Atzerodt was known as "Port Tobacco," and Powell was known as either "Baptist Minister" or "Wood."

The plan as originally hatched by John Wilkes Booth, was to kidnap Lincoln, and whisk him off to Richmond. Once there he assumed the South could exchange Lincoln for the freedom of all Southern soldiers held by the Union, or some other bounty beneficial to the Confederacy.

To this end Booth and his fellow conspirators, Samuel Arnold and Michael O' Laughlen, assembled together on March 17th, 1865, planning to kidnap the President while he was on his way to watch the play, "Still Waters Run Deep" at the Campbell Military Hospital.

The plan was to stop his coach just outside of Washington. John Surratt was to drive the coach, as he was most familiar with the area. Once they were far enough out of sight they intended to abandon the coach. To this end Booth had relays of horses lined up along the route to Port Tobacco. At Port Tobacco, he had a boat waiting to make their escape.

The plan however was foiled when Lincoln cancelled his plans instead attending a ceremony to honor the 142nd Indiana Infantry at the National Hotel. Ironically Booth was then staying at the National Hotel, and if he had remained there, he may have been able to carry out his plan at that time.

***

Still another plot hatched by Booth about this same time was to kidnap Lincoln during a performance at Ford's Theater. This plan involved Booth, Samuel Arnold, and George A. Atzerodt. In preparation Booth had rented a stable in the rear of the theater. The plan was for Arnold to rush into the President's Box and seize Lincoln, while Booth and Atzerodt were to handcuff the President and lower him to the stage. At this point the lights were supposed to be lowered, allowing them to rush out of the rear entrance and make their escape on horses they had waiting there.

A similar plot had them kidnapping Lincoln on one of his regular unescorted walks to the War Department. Once they had him, it was thought they could hold him prisoner in Van Ness House, until they could arrange their escape, or make a beneficial arrangement with the Union Government.

Booth Sets His Mind on Assassination

Before April 11th all of Booth's plans had one element in common – kidnapping President Lincoln. But a speech given by Lincoln that day changed everything. According to David Herold, who was in the audience with Booth, Booth became outraged with Lincoln's message that he favored the "elective franchise for the colored man."

Herold says Booth grasped his shoulder excitedly saying, "That means Nigger Citizenship! Now, by ------ I'll put him through!"

John Wilkes Booth

The Fateful Day

THE ASSASSINATION OF PRESIDENT LINCOLN

April 14th, 1865, found Washington, D.C. in a celebratory mood. Robert E. Lee had surrendered to General Ulysses S. Grant just five days before. Grant the conquering hero was visiting town, and people everywhere were trying to get a glimpse of him.

That same morning Mary Lincoln booked a box for herself, the President, and General Grant and his wife at Ford's Theater. The play that night, "Our American Cousin" featured actress Laura Keene.

Theater owner, John Ford, placed notices in the paper that the President would be attending the performance that night, and it was expected to draw a large audience, because so many people wanted to get a glimpse of General Grant.

That same morning, John Wilkes Booth stopped by Ford's Theater to pick up his mail that had been delivered there. At that time he learned that the President would be in attendance that night, and he began his plotting anew.

Ford's brother, Harry Ford, at once set about having the theater decorated for the President's visit. He had the partition removed that separated the two boxes the Presidential party would occupy. Two flags were draped across the front and sides of the box, and more comfortable furniture was exchanged for the furniture normally in the booth. For President Lincoln, they brought in an upholstered rocking chair normally used in Harry Ford's sleeping room.

Unknown to everyone, one of the helpers, Edmund Spangler, helped bring about the success of the assassination plot. While he was setting up the Presidential Box, Spangler dug, and chipped a hole in one of the doors. It was through this hole that Booth was able to spy inside the box. He also left the board that Booth used to secure the door after he entered the President's Box.

At the same time, Booth continued devising his plan to cripple the government. Killing the President was only beginning of his design. The plan as he conceived it was to eliminate the top three people in the Government, effectively throwing the Government into chaos, thus giving the Confederacy a chance to regroup.

He came very close to succeeding.

■■

Mary Todd Lincoln, wife of Abraham Lincoln

About midday, General Grant and Mrs. Grant, canceled out on the theater party, deciding instead to visit their children in Burlington, New Jersey. Mrs. Lincoln then chose Major Henry R. Rathbone and Miss Clara Harris, the daughter of Senator Harris to replace the Grant's.

President Lincoln continued on with his business seeing visitors at the White House up until the time of their departure for the theater.

The Presidential Party arrived at Ford's Theater around 8:30 PM. According to William Withers, Jr. the orchestra leader, they played "Hail to the Chief" as the Lincoln's entered the theater. The crowd stood up over and over again cheering for the President. They waved handkerchiefs and hats to salute him. As Lincoln entered the Presidential Box he smiled down at the audience and bowed to the crowd before being seated.

The President was seated in the rocker close to the balcony. Mrs. Lincoln was in the arm chair next to him. Miss Harris was at the far right, and just behind her Major Rathbone was seated on the sofa.

***

John Wilkes Booth had a hurried day as he worked to bring his plans to culmination.

According to John Buckingham, the night door keeper at Ford's Theater, Booth was in and out of the theater at least five times that day. But no one saw anything unusual in this as Booth had unlimited access to the theater, and was good friends with the theater owner, John Ford.

Around midday Booth attempted to visit Vice-President Andrew Johnson at Kirkwood House, handing the doorman his calling card, and saying he knew the Vice-President. The thought is that he was trying to learn the layout of the room so he could relay that information to George A. Atzerodt, whose part in the conspiracy was to kill the Vice-President.

Later that day when Booth passed his key to the clerk of the National Hotel he asked him "Are you going down to Ford's Theater Tonight?" The clerk answered "No." Booth is said to have replied, "You ought to go, there is to be some splendid acting tonight."

Samuel Arnold

Killing President Lincoln

Mary E. Surratt, hung for her part in the conspiracy

The next time Booth was spotted was at ten minutes past ten.

He was seen drinking a brandy at an adjoining saloon on the south side of the theater. Shortly after this he encountered John Buckingham as he entered Ford's Theater. He asked Buckingham for the time, and made his way towards the stairs.

He passed around the dress circle moving towards the door leading to the President's Box. His movements were not unseen. According to William Withers, Jr., he saw Booth walking in the balcony, moving towards the President's Box, but he thought nothing of it as Booth was a normal visitor at the theater.

Lincoln's bodyguard that night was John Parker, an undistinguished Washington, D.C. policeman. Parker was supposed to be stationed in the little passageway outside of the entrance to the Presidential Box guarding Lincoln. Apparently Parker abandoned his post several times during the performance, once to watch the play from the first gallery, and after the intermission he disappeared altogether with Lincoln's footman and coachman to visit a nearby tavern.

As a result, the Presidential Box was left unattended when Booth arrived.

Booth crept in through the unguarded door. After entering the passageway to the Presidential Box, he grabbed the block of wood Spangler left there for him, and barred the doorway shut. From here he moved down the passageway, coming upon the two doors to the box Lincoln was in. Normally when the President was in attendance these doors were kept locked, but for some unknown reason, they were unlocked upon Booth's arrival. Chances are that Booth took a moment to steady himself, and that he peered into the President's Box, looking through the peep hole that Spangler had chiseled into it for him.

Michael O'Laughlen

At 10:20 PM Booth peeked in through the door with his Derringer raised and leveled. He fired a ball into the back of President Lincoln's head. Lincoln slumped forward, motionless.

Inside the box it was clouded with white smoke from the powder and shot. Mary Lincoln let out a screech when she realized what happened. Major Henry A. Rathbone jumped to his feet and began struggling with Booth. Booth lashed out at him with his dagger. He thrust at Rathbone's heart. Moving quickly Rathbone parried the blow with his arm. The dagger dug several inches deep into his arm, and tore into his chest.

Booth broke free and attempted to escape. Rathbone grasped at Booth's coat, but didn't have the strength to hold him, and Booth managed to break free again. Booth jumped to the stage, catching his leg in the draped flags as he leapt.

Wither's testimony gives a vivid account of what followed.

He "heard the crack of a revolver," as he was returning to the orchestra. "I saw a man jump from the President's Box onto the stage. He ran directly to the door leading to the back stage. This course brought him right in my pathway. He had a dagger in his hand, and he waved it threateningly. He slashed at me, and the knife cut through my coat, vest, and underclothing. He struck again, the point of the weapon penetrating the back of my neck, and the blow brought me to the floor. I recognized him as J. Wilkes Booth, and watched him make his exit to the alley."

Another witness to the scene, a Miss Porterfield, was attending the play with her mother. Her story was revealed in a 1913 issue of Century Magazine.

"We heard the report of a pistol-shot, followed almost immediately by Booth's dramatic leap from the President's Box. I remember distinctly the gleam of his dagger as he descended to the stage. I heard him shout something ... I could not clearly distinguish his words, of course later they were [known] "sic semper tyrannis!" "The South is avenged!"

Looking up to the box, "I could not see the President, but I could see Mrs. Lincoln and hear her shrieks and moans."

In the confusion, most people thought it was all part of the play – the shot (if they heard it at all) and Booth's dramatic leap to the stage.

***

After making his way to the alley, Booth grabbed the reigns to his horse from John Burroughs, knocking him to the ground, after bludgeoning him on the head with the butt of his knife. He made his escape rushing through the streets of the Capitol.

***

In the President's Box, Major Rathbone pulled himself up, and unbarred the door to let help in. Miss Harris told them "The President is shot."

Charles P. Taft, a surgeon, who was in the audience that night, approached the stage. Onlookers helped to lift him up into the box. By this time other doctors arrived through the upstairs door to the box, and they began trying to assess the President's situation.

At first the doctors thought the President had been stabbed or wounded in the chest. They lifted him to the floor, and began stripping off his clothes. Moments later they discovered that he was shot in the head. The ball had entered the back of his head behind the left ear and was embedded in his brain.

Once they discovered the source of the wound, they were determined to remove Lincoln to the nearest bed and do whatever they could to comfort him. The President was carried out of the theater. A man across the street invited them in to use his room, so they carried the President in, and laid him on the bed. According to Taft it was a gruesome scene. As they carried Lincoln, "blood [was] dripping from the wound, faster and faster."

Inside Petersen House a vigil was held over the dying Lincoln. Surgeon Charles Taft spent most of the night holding the President's head so blood and brain tissue could continue to ooze out, and prevent clotting. He was relieved several times in his task by another surgeon, Charles H. Crane.

Lincoln passed away at 7:22 the next morning, April 15th, 1865.

They wrapped his body in a flag taken from the Tenth Street House, and carried him through the streets of Washington, D.C., returning him to the White House. As they walked along, they noticed that flags were already lowered to half-mast in honor of the dead president. Once at the White House the body was carried to a guest room. It was prepared for showing, and there Lincoln lay in State for three days while mourners coursed through to view the dead President.

Lewis Powell (AKA Lewis Payne)

Treachery in the Night

Lincoln wasn't the only target that night.

A similar plot was unfolding at the home of Secretary of State, William H. Seward. Lewis Thornton Powell rang the bell of the Seward Mansion about 10:00 PM. He told the doorkeeper that he was delivering medicine for Seward. After some argument Powell was allowed to take the medicine upstairs.

At the top of the stairs he was confronted by Frederick Seward, a son of Secretary Seward, who sent Powell away. Powell started down the stairs, then turned around and attacked Frederick Seward with the butt of his revolver. Upon hearing the commotion Seward's nurse assistant, Sergeant George E. Robinson, came rushing out to help. Powell struck him in the forehead with his knife, and raced to Secretary Seward's bed, where he stabbed him in the neck three times with his dagger.

Ironically Seward's life was probably saved by the fact that he'd been in a carriage accident several days before in which he broke his arm and fractured his jaw. The steel brace his doctor had placed on his neck and jaw deflected some of the pressure from Powell's knife, thus saving his life.

As Powell was getting ready to strike at Seward again, Sergeant Robinson and Major August H. Seward (another son of the Secretary) pulled him away. Powell struggled, broke free, and made his escape, stabbing a messenger on his way out of the house.

Alone, and without assistance Powell hid out in a nearby cemetery for three days. Not knowing where to meet up with his fellow conspirators, he decided to return to the one place he knew they frequented, Mary Surratt's Washington boarding house. Unfortunately, his timing could not have been worse. At the time he arrived there, authorities were searching the boarding house.

Both Lewis Powell and Mary Surratt were taken into custody there.

***

About this same time George A. Atzerodt, another conspirator, was lodging at Kirkwood House. His room was just below that of Vice-President Andrew Johnson. Atzerodt was entrusted with the job of killing the Vice-President.

Atzerodt ended up getting drunk instead, and wandering the streets of Washington. Atzerodt gave himself away at a tavern by asking the bartender where the President was sleeping. The bartender found the request suspicious after hearing about Lincoln's assassination and the attack on Seward. He immediately contacted the police, and gave them information that led to Atzerodt's arrest.

When his room was searched it was found that he had not slept in it. Police found a bank book belonging to John Wilkes Booths, a map of Virginia, and under his pillow they found a revolver that was loaded and capped.

He was apprehended at his cousin's house in Germantown, Maryland on April 20th, 1865.

***

Michael O'Laughlen boarded Grant's train to Philadelphia on the afternoon of April 14th, 1865 with the intent of killing him. He was prevented from getting access to Grant's private car because it was locked and guarded by porters.

Pursuit and Capture of the Conspirators

As word filtered in about Lincoln's assassination and the attack on Seward, Washington was thrown into a panic.

Martial law was declared.

Every exit to the city was guarded. Outgoing trains were stopped and searched. Mounted police and cavalry patrolled the streets. Nearby forts were put on alert, and the guns were manned waiting for a possible Confederate attack.

A massive manhunt was mounted to search out the conspirators. Secretary of War Edwin Stanton placed a $100,000 reward on the heads of the conspirators.

Earlier on the day of Lincoln's assassination Booth had met with Mary Surratt twice at her Washington home. That morning he gave her his field glasses, and orders to get things ready for his getaway. Mrs. Surratt and Lewis Weichmann immediately set off for Surratt's Tavern in Surrattsville, about twelve miles south of Washington. Once there she let the tavern keeper know that two gentlemen would come that night. He was to have two carbines, Booth's field glasses, and two bottles of whiskey ready for them when they arrived.

Later that afternoon Booth met with Mary Surratt once again to confirm that his supplies would be waiting.

***

John Wilkes Booth and David Herold met up at Surrat's Tavern shortly after midnight on the night of the assassination.

They were next seen at the home of Dr. Samuel Mudd. Herold approached Mudd and told him that "while riding rapidly [Booth's] horse had fallen on him and broke his leg." Mudd dressed the wounded leg. That night Booth and Herold stayed with Dr. Mudd and his wife. They left about 4:00 PM the next afternoon.

Sunday morning Booth and Herold arrived at the home of Captain Samuel Cox, a Southern sympathizer. Booth convinced Cox to help them cross the Potomac. Cox was at first reluctant, but eventually instructed them to hide in the nearby pine thickets. Later Cox returned with food, and guided them to the home of Thomas A. Jones, who lived at a place called Huckleberry.

Jones cared for them almost a week, biding his time for the right opportunity to take them across the Potomac. On the night of Friday, April 21, Jones placed Booth upon his horse, and led the two men to the river, where he had a boat waiting for them to make their escape.

That same day Booth wrote in his diary:

> *"After being hunted like a dog through swamp, woods, and last night being chased by gunboats until I was forced to return, wet, cold, and starving with everyman's hand against me, I am here in despair. And why? – for doing what Brutus was honored for – what made Tell a hero. And yet I, for striking down a greater tyrant than they ever knew, am looked upon as a common cut throat. My action was purer than either of theirs…I have to great a soul to die like a criminal…"*

Saturday, a Negro, saw the fugitives hiding out along the river, and reported their whereabouts to detectives.

Unaware that they were seen, Booth and Herold proceeded towards Bowling Green, ending up at the farm of Jack Garrett.

News of Lincoln's assassination had not reached the area yet, so Garrett was completely unaware of whom Booth was. Garrett fed the two men, and let them spend the night in his barn.

The 16th New York Cavalry that had been pursuing the conspirators arrived at Garrett's farm just after midnight on April 26th. They were led by Lieutenant Edward P. Doherty. After questioning Garrett about his two visitors, Doherty sent him into the barn to tell the two men to surrender.

Garrett informed the two men that soldiers would fire the barn if they did not surrender. Booth responded that he would rather fight, but said, "...there is a man in here who does want to surrender pretty bad." Herold was allowed to leave the barn.

Lieutenant Doherty then had Garrett pile brush around the barn, and proceeded to set it on fire. And, overanxious soldier fired on Booth. He was struck in the spine, and fell flat on his face. Soldiers rushed in to the burning barn to pull him out, and carried the wounded Booth to Garrett's porch.

According to Sergeant Boston Corbett who shot and killed Booth:

> *When the fire started [Booth] "was standing in the middle of the barn, and I supposed he was going to fight his way out. I became convinced it was time for me to shoot, and I took a steady aim on my arm with my revolver and, through a large crack in the barn shot him ... the wound was made in the neck, back of the ear, and came out a little higher up, on the other side of the head."*

Booth was shot at 3:15 AM on April 26th, 1865, and took two hours to die, a painful excruciating death. His last words were, "Tell my mother I died for my country and ... I did what I thought was best." Later he muttered – "Useless. Useless." And then he expired.

On his person, they discovered three revolvers, a dagger, and a slung-shot.

Funeral of Abraham Lincoln

Fate of the Conspirators

- Edmund Spangler was sentenced to 6 years at hard labor. He was pardoned by President Andrew Johnson on March 1, 1869.
- Samuel Arnold was sentenced to life in prison at hard labor. He was pardoned by President Andrew Johnson on March 1, 1869.
- Michael O'Laughlen was sentenced to life in prison at hard labor. He died two years later in prison at Fort Jefferson during an outbreak of yellow fever

- Dr. Samuel Mudd was sentenced to life at hard labor, but was pardoned in March of 1869 for his part in helping quell a yellow fever outbreak at the prison.
- Mary Surratt was found guilty for her part in the plot, and was sentenced to death. She was hung with fellow conspirators on July 7, 1865. Mary Surratt has the dubious honor of being the first woman executed by the Federal Government.
- Lewis Powell was sentenced to death. He was hung with fellow conspirators on July 7, 1865.
- David Herold was sentenced to death. He was hung with fellow conspirators on July 7, 1865.
- George Atzerodt was sentenced to death. He was hung with fellow conspirators on July 7, 1865.

John Surratt was the only one of the main conspirators not to be convicted.

At the time of the President's assassination he was in Elmira, New York, on secret service for the Confederate Government. After hearing about the assassination he fled to Canada, and stayed there until the other conspirators were executed in July of 1867. He traveled to England in 1865, and then on to Rome where he became a member of the Papal Zouaves. He managed to escape when secret service agents arrested him in Rome, and was later arrested in Alexandria, Egypt.

After being returned to the United States, he stood trial for his part in the assassination conspiracy, being tried in a civilian court, not a military court, as the other conspirators were. The trial ended on August 10, of 1867 with a hung jury. The government dropped all charges against Surratt, and he was set free in the summer of 1868.

In 1870 he went on a lecture tour discussing his part in the Abraham Lincoln conspiracy. It was short lived however, as people were repulsed by his trying to making money on the President's death. His tour was cancelled after just one speech.

James Garfield

The President's carriage arrived at the Baltimore and Potomac Railway Station about 9:20 AM on Saturday morning, July 2, 1881.

With him was James G. Blaine, Secretary of State. Inside the station, Garfield and Blaine were talking near the ladies waiting room. About 9:30 AM the crack of a pistol sounded through the depot, closely followed by a second shot.

According to a witness, Miss Ella M. Ridgely,

> "The first shot was fired, and then [Guiteau] took two or three steps nearer to the President and fired a second shot when about four feet from him. On the first shot the President threw up his hands and

> *fell back. He kept sinking all the time as the second shot was fired."*

The President fell to the floor, blood spurting profusely from the jagged wound in his side.

The Shooter, Charles J. Guiteau, described the scene like this:

> *I "was about three or four feet from the door. I stood five or six feet behind him, right in the middle of the room, and as he was walking away from me, I pulled out the revolver and fired. He straightened up and threw his head back and seemed to be perfectly bewildered. He did not seem to know what struck him. I looked at him; he did not drop; I thereupon pulled again. He dropped his head, seemed to reel, and fell over."*

Blaine left the President's side pursuing the shooter. In no time, he returned to find the President lying on the floor. A woman who had been standing nearby was on the floor beside the President resting his head upon her knee.

White smoke from the powder and shot filled the area around the president. Guiteau slipped the gun back into his pocket as he headed for the exit where he had a cab waiting to whisk him away. Policeman, Patrick Kearney was stationed outside the depot. He heard two shots, but had no idea that the President had been shot. He detained Guiteau as he was leaving the station.

Guiteau immediately started proclaiming, "I did it; I will go to jail for it. Arthur is President and I am a stalwart."

Assassination of President Garfield

At the police station, a search of Guiteau found a cache of his personal papers, the revolver he used to shoot the

President with, and a copy of his book, *The Truth*, upon his person.

Guiteau boasted from his jail cell that what he did was for the good of the nation, and he eagerly awaited news of Garfield's death. His arrogance brought about numerous death threats, and soldiers and police guarded his cell constantly to keep the mob from lynching him. On September 11th, 1881, one of his guards, William Mason, attempted to kill him. Only the iron bars of the cell saved his life, and the bullet ended up just grazing Guiteau's head.

When questioned about why he tried to kill the President, Guiteau responded:

> *"I think of General Garfield's condition as a removal, not an assassination. My idea was, simply stated, to remove as easily as possible Mr. James A. Garfield, a quiet good-natured citizen of Ohio, who temporarily occupied the position of President of the United States, and substitute in his place Mr. Chester A. Arthur [the Vice-President].*
>
> *"The President's nomination was an act of God, his election was an act of God, and his removal is an act of God."*

The President's suffering

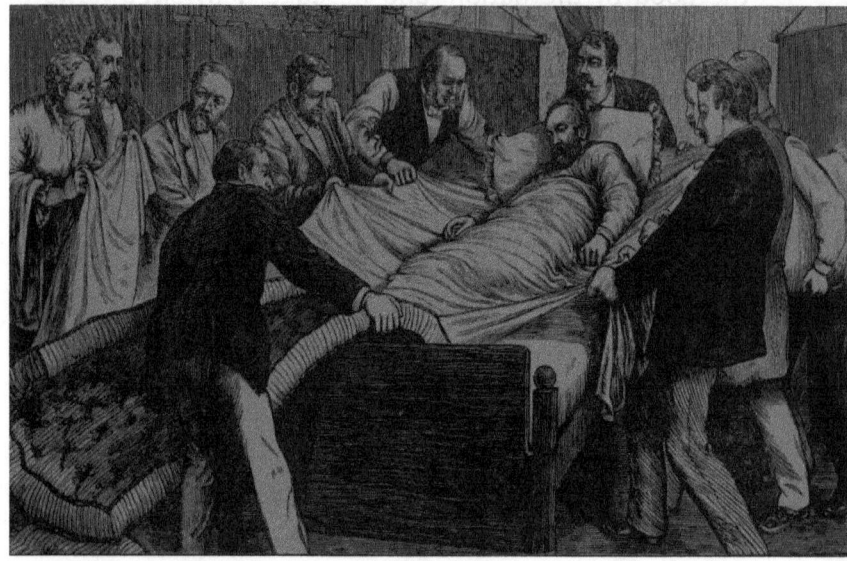

President Garfield in his sick bed surrounded by his physicians

At first the doctor's considered the wound to be mortal.

A surgeon who had been waiting outside of the railroad station initially cared for the President. Onlookers removed a mattress from one of the train cars, and placed Garfield upon it. At the President's order, he was rushed by ambulance to the White House where more doctors were called in to assess his situation.

Mrs. Garfield, who was waiting for the President at Long Branch, New Jersey, was taken back to Washington by a special train. The news she received was grim at best. Doctors were sure the wound was fatal, and offered little hope that the President would make it through the night. After he survived the first night doctors became more hopeful that he might recover.

And, thus began the long summer of 1881.

Garfield continued to hang on through the summer. He remained conscious, and was often in great pain. His body was racked by fevers. He had trouble eating, and could often only hold down liquids. During the course of his illness he lost over one hundred pounds. Doctors probed his body repeatedly, and could not uncover the bullet that was still lodged inside him. Medicine at the time contributed to the President's growing weakness. The doctors probed and dug for the lost bullet using unsterilized fingers and instruments. As a result infection spread though Garfield's body making him sicker.

The weather in Washington was hot and sticky all summer. Garfield's sick room became a prison of sweat and pain. Navy engineer's constructed a makeshift air conditioner, blowing air over ice to bring him some relief. Inventor Alexander Graham Bell, of telephone fame, built a metal detector to help doctors find the bullet buried deep inside the President's body. It was no help in finding the bullet.

On September 6th it was decided to move Garfield from the White House, thinking a change of temperature and scenery would help to improve his condition. To accomplish this huge task with minimal discomfort to the President special railroad tracks were built leading to the White House, and another set was built leading to Francklyn Cottage in Long Branch, New Jersey, where the President would be staying.

Garfield passed away two weeks later at 10:35 PM on September 19th, 1881. He was just fifty years old.

Today it is generally agreed that the wound was not fatal. The state of medicine in that day and age was the immediate cause of death. His doctor's had guessed wrong about the path of the bullet and were looking for it in the wrong place. Their probing with unsterilized fingers and instruments caused the infection that poisoned the President's body and eventually killed him.

Charles J. Guiteau – Assassin

Charles Julius Guiteau

Guiteau was a lawyer originally from Freeport, Illinois. Most of his life was spent drifting from place to place. As a young man he had been a member of the Oneida Community (a religious sect). From there he moved to Chicago, Boston, and New York – failing at all of the tasks he attempted. In 1875 his family had tried to commit him as insane, but he got away before they could complete the process.

He spent the months prior to the assassination politicking in New York. His claim to "fame" was a speech he had written titled "Garfield Against Hancock." Somehow Guiteau got permission to give his speech to a small group of blacks. He considered the speech a political masterpiece that was instrumental in getting Garfield elected to the Presidency. One of the New York party leaders speaking at Guiteau's trial said the speech was nonsense, and everyone there treated Guiteau like a "laughing stock."

After the election Guiteau moved to Washington and began dogging the President. He constantly touted his speech in missives to Garfield and Secretary of State James G. Blaine. He began asking first for the Austrian Mission, and when that was given to William Walter Phelps he set his course upon the Paris Mission.

He apparently went around the city telling landlords and any other people who would listen to him that Garfield had promised him the Paris Mission. In his autobiography he said, "The case was pending at the time I shot the President, and, as I before stated I confidently expected a favorable answer." He went on to say that the shooting was not about this, he did it "under Divine Pressure."

He followed the President around Washington waiting for an opportunity to talk with him about the Consulship. He visited the White House often, and each time was told Garfield was out, or too busy to see him. He dogged Blaine, until Blaine finally told him, "Never bother me again about the Paris Consulship."

Eventually Garfield tired of Guiteau's visits, and he ordered White House officers to "refuse him admittance should he attempt to enter again."

According to Guiteau, the idea of killing the President came to him like this:

> "I was in my bed ... and I was thinking over the political situation, and the idea flashed through my brain that if the President was out of the way everything would go better ... the only way to unite the two factions of the Republican party, and save the Republic from going into the hands of the rebels and Democrats, was to quickly remove the President."

To put his plan into action Guiteau borrowed $15.00 from an old friend, George C. Maynard, telling him he needed the money for rent, and other such necessities. With that money he visited O'Mera's Store in Washington, and purchased a pearl handled revolver, bullets, and a ladies pen knife with $10.00 of the money.

From that point on he was constantly following the President, devising how and when to "remove" him.

One such plot had Guiteau following the President from the White House to Blaine's Home. Outside the house, he had his gun cocked and ready to shoot, but couldn't work up the nerve to pull the trigger.

Another time he went to the train station saying, "I went to the station all prepared to remove him." He got to the depot about 9:00 AM, and waited outside for the President's carriage to arrive. At 9:25 AM the President arrived. According to Guiteau, he couldn't do it this time because "Mrs. Garfield looked so thin, and she clung so tenderly to the President's arm, that I did not have the heart to fire on him."

A week before the shooting he followed Garfield to Church, saying "I intended to shoot him through the head and let the ball pass through the ceiling, in order that no one else should be injured." Once again he couldn't bring himself to pull the trigger. He left, promising himself he "would certainly do it the next Sunday."

Guiteau was carrying the following letter addressed to the White House at the time he shot the President:

> July 2nd, 1881
>
> To the White House:
>
> The President's tragic death was a sad necessity, but it will unite the Republican Party and save the Republic. Life is a flimsy dream, and it matters little when one goes. A human life is of small value. During the war thousands of brave boys went down without a tear.
>
> I presume the President was a Christian, and that he will be happier in Paradise than here. It will be no worse for Mrs. Garfield, dear soul, to part with her husband this way than by natural death. He is liable to go at any time, anyway. I had no ill-will toward the President. His death was a political necessity.
>
> I am a lawyer, a theologian, and a politician. I am a Stalwart of Stalwarts. I was with General Grant and the rest of our men, in New York, during the canvass. I have some papers for the press, for which I will leave with

> Byron Andrews, and his co-journalists, at 1420 New York Avenue, where all the reporters can see them. I am going to the jail.
>
> Charles Guiteau

Another letter written by Guiteau was found outside of the railroad station. It was written to General William Tecumseh Sherman, and read as follows:

To General Sherman:

> I have just shot the President. I have shot him several times, as I wished him to go as easily as possible. His death was a political necessity. I am a lawyer, theologian, and politician. I am a Stalwart of Stalwarts. I was with General Grant and the rest of our men, in New York during the canvass. I am going to jail. Please send out your troops, and take possession of the jail at once.

Trial of Charles J. Guiteau

Police van transporting Guiteau to the Court House

Guiteau's erratic actions during the course of his trial made him a media sensation.

On Friday October 14th, 1881 Guiteau was brought to court and arraigned on charges of killing the President.

He plead not guilty on three counts:

1) Insanity. "It was God's act, not mine."
2) The President died from malpractice, not from his bullet. Thus his doctors killed him.
3) Lack of jurisdiction.

The trial began on November 14th, 1881, and lasted just over three months. George M. Scoville, the brother-in-law of Charles J. Guiteau, acted as counsel for defense.

Scoville was battling Guiteau through most of the trial, trying to run the case the way he thought best. He decided to ignore the other two pleas, and focus on the insanity defense.

Both, Scoville and the district attorney, dragged in a slew of witnesses from Guiteau's troubled past. They also, each had a large number of doctors and psychologists to testify on whether Guiteau was insane or not.

During the trial Guiteau insisted, "It was on the inspiration of the Deity. I never would have shot the President on my own personal account."

When asked, "You did not succeed in the Divine Will?" he responded, "I think the doctors finished the work."

The questioning continued:

Question: "Did you believe it was the Will of God that you should murder the President?"

Answer: "I believed that it was His will that he should be removed, and I was appointed the agent to do it."

Question: "Did he give you a commission in writing?"

Answer: "No sir."

Question: "Did he give it to you audibly?"

Answer: "No sir."

Question: "He did not come to you as a vision in the night?"

Answer: "I do not get my inspiration in that way."

Later in the trial Guiteau added more shocking anecdotes.

When asked again, why he removed (Guiteau would not say kill or murder) the President, he responded, It is "not that Guiteau loved Garfield less, but that he loved his country more."

On another occasion when he was speaking during the trial he explained:

> "I presume I shall live to be President. Some people think I am as a good man as the President (Chester A. Arthur) now.
>
> Providence and I saved the nation, and why should I not be a hero and the equal of Washington, Lincoln, and Grant?"

When the trial was finished Judge Cox gave lengthy instructions to the jury explaining the insanity defense and how it should be interpreted. The jury was sequestered. After only twenty minutes of deliberation, they returned the verdict of "guilty!"

When the verdict of guilty was read out, Guiteau screamed,

"My blood will be upon the heads of that jury; don't you forget it."

"God will avenge this outrage!"

Judge Cox sentenced him to execution by hanging on June 30th, 1882.

In a final attempt to save his life Guiteau plead his case to President Chester A. Arthur in this letter:

> *I am entitled to a full pardon; but I am willing to wait for the public to be educated up to my views and feelings in the matter. In the meantime I suffer in bonds as a patriot...I am willing to DIE for my inspiration, but it will make a terrible reckoning for you and this nation. I made you, and saved the American people great trouble. And the least you can do is let me go; but I appreciate your delicate position, and I am willing to stay here until January, if necessary. I am God's man in this matter. This is dead sure.*

It was to no avail. Charles Julius Guiteau entered the executioner's stand on June 30, 1882, and was hanged by the neck until dead. After a half hour dangling by the rope, his body was taken down and placed in a waiting coffin.

Guiteau in corridor of jail looking at executioner's rope

William McKinley

Temple of Music at Pan-American Exposition

The Temple of Music was the most ornately decorated building at the Pan-American Exposition. It spanned 150 feet on each side, and the dome rose 180 feet into the air. Outside the primary color was red, trimmed with yellow and gold. Inside, the ceiling dome was blue green. It boasted one of the largest pipe organs in the United States, and had seating for 2200 people. Each corner featured statues designed by Isidore Konti. And, at night it offered a brilliant display of electrical illumination.

At 4:07 PM on September 21st, 1901, two gun shots rang out through the Temple of Music striking President William McKinley.

An eyewitness, John D. Wells, writing in Collier's Magazine gave this account of the shooting:

> "Suddenly I saw a hand shoved toward the President – two of them in fact – as if the person wished to grasp the President's hand in both of his own. In the palm of one hand, the right one, was a handkerchief. Then there were two shots in rapid succession.
>
> "I stood stock still. I saw Detective Foster strike upward the hand that would fire the third shot, and a soldier seize the man from behind and drag him down."
>
> The President "fell into the arms of Detective Geary. Mr. Milburn supported him from the other side. Just a few drops of blood spurted out and dropped on his white waistcoat."
>
> Seconds later "I rushed to where the assassin lay prostate on the floor. A dozen or more men, detectives and guards, were standing over him, striking and kicking him."
>
> The President observing the rough treatment being given the shooter, told nearby officers, "See that no one hurts him."

This follows pretty closely the other accounts of the assassination.

Assassination of President McKinley, Pan-American Exposition

Leon Czolgosz waited in line for his turn to shake hands with the President. In front of him, a man took his little daughter up to meet the President. The President shook her hand, and watched as she walked away.

The man in front of Czolgosz was a short Italian type. He was about 26 years old, with dark shaggy brows, and a black mustache. He aroused the suspicion of detectives because he held the President's hand for an overlong time. Detectives rushed forward and pulled him away.

Next in line was Leon Czolgosz. He made his way towards the President, his left hand extended to shake the President's hand When there was less than a foot between them – Czolgosz fired into the President.

After the first shot McKinley rose up on his toes, and made a gasping sound. The President turned slightly to the left. The second shot entered his body just below the navel. McKinley bent over slightly and began to fall backwards. Secret Service Agent Geary and Exposition President John G. Milburn caught the President.

As Geary caught the President, McKinley asked, "Am I shot?" Geary unbuttoned the President's vest, seeing the blood seeping through, and said, "I fear you are, Mr. President."

A Negro waiter, James F. Parker, described as 6 foot 4 inches tall, and weighing 250 pounds, attacked the assassin, knocking him to the floor. Seconds later Czolgosz was surrounded by Exposition Police and Secret Service Agents.

Detectives moved McKinley to a chair until medical help could be found. An ambulance from the Exposition was used to move the President to the onsite hospital where they could further examine his wounds. Presidential Secretary George Cortelyou and Exposition President John G. Milburn accompanied McKinley in the ambulance.

James Parker, the man who tackled McKinley's assassin

Outside news of the assassination quickly spread among the waiting crowd of over fifty thousand people. There was much talk of lynching the assassin. Someone went so far as to take the rope from a flag pole in the esplanade.

Inside Czolgosz was dragged to a side room of the Temple of Music moving him further away from the mob. He was badly beaten at the hands of the detectives and there was some question whether he would survive.

When questioned, all Leon Czolgosz would tell authorities was that his name was "Nieman" (an alias that he had used before) and that he "was an anarchist, and he had done his duty."

President McKinley falling into arms of George Cortelyou

The Assassin's statement

Leon Czolgosz, President McKinley's assassin

At the Police station Leon Czolgosz gave the following statement detailing his actions:

Question: "Did you mean to kill the President?"

Answer: "I did."

Question: "What was the motive that induced you to commit this crime?

Answer: "I am a disciple of Emma Goldman."

He had been friends with anarchists in Chicago, Cleveland, and Detroit.

What follows is taken from Czolgosz's signed statement given to detectives.

"Eight days ago, while I was in Chicago, I read in a Chicago newspaper of President McKinley's visit to the Pan-American Exposition at Buffalo. That day I bought a ticket and got here with the determination to do something, but I did not know just what. I thought of shooting the President, but I had not formed a plan.

"Not until Tuesday morning did the resolution to shoot the President take hold of me. It was in my heart; there was no escape for me. I could not have conquered it had my life been at stake. There were thousands of people in town on Tuesday. I heard it was President's day. All these people seemed bowing to the great ruler. I made up my mind to kill that ruler. I bought a 32 caliber revolver and loaded it.

"What started the craze to kill was a lecture I heard some little time ago by Emma Goldman. She set me on fire. Her doctrine that all rulers should be exterminated was what set me to thinking so that my head nearly split.

"On Tuesday night I went to the fair grounds and was near the railroad gate when the Presidential party arrived. I tried to get near him, but the police forced me back. They forced everybody back so that the great ruler could pass. I was close to the President when he got into the grounds, but was afraid to attempt the assassination because there were so many men in the bodyguard that watched him."

Wednesday he returned to the Exposition waiting for an opportunity to shoot the President. "I thought half a dozen times of shooting while he was speaking, but I could not get close enough."

Thursday was the same. "I waited near the central entrance for the President who was to board his special train from that gate, but the police allowed nobody but the President's party to pass where the train waited."

On Friday, the day of the assassination, he says:

"During yesterday I first thought of hiding my pistol under my handkerchief. I was afraid if I had to draw it from my pocket I would be seen and seized by the guards. I got to the Temple of Music the first one and waited at the spot where the reception was to be held.

"Then he came, the President – the ruler – and I got in line and trembled and trembled until I got right up to him, and then I shot him twice through my white handkerchief. I would have fired more, but I was stunned by a blow in the face – a frightful blow that knocked me down – and then everybody jumped on me. I thought I would be killed and was surprised the way they treated me.

"I had no confidants; no one to help me. I was alone, absolutely."

The suffering President

Theodore Roosevelt being sworn in as President

President McKinley lived six and one half days after being shot.

McKinley was conscious all of the time after being shot. Inside the Exposition Hospital it was determined to operate on the President. All of the arrangements fell to the President's Secretary, George Cortelyou, who accompanied him that day.

When doctors undressed the President for surgery, the first bullet fell out of his jacket as they were taking it off of him. It had struck the button of McKinley's jacket, and gone into him just above the breastbone, but not deep.

The second bullet entered the President's abdomen, five inches below the left nipple. The bullet hole going in was small and clean, but the hole on the other side was large and ragged.

The actual surgery lasted one hour. It was discovered that "this hole, where the bullet went out of the stomach, was larger than the hole in the front wall of the stomach; in fact, it was a wound over an inch in diameter, jagged and ragged. It was sewed up in three layers." The surgeons found it necessary to turn up the stomach. Doctors were hopeful, because it appeared none of the contents of the stomach had entered the abdominal cavity. Because of this, they felt sure that peritonitis (infection) would not be an issue.

On Saturday, the day following the shooting, McKinley was holding his own. All of his vitals looked good. Most of his doctors were still uncertain about the fate of the President, and were waiting to see what Sunday brought before making a final prognosis. Doctor P. M. Rixey was the only one of McKinley's physicians who publicly said he felt the President would recover.

After the surgery, McKinley was removed to the home of Pan-American Exposition President John Milburn. It was here that doctors attended him daily, and cabinet members filed through to pay respects to the wounded President.

Vice-President Theodore Roosevelt rushed to Buffalo to visit with the ailing President. By Tuesday the President was doing so well, Roosevelt left on a hunting trip for the Adirondacks. Other visitors to the Milburn home included Senator Hanna, and Abner McKinley, the President's brother.

An X-ray machine had been brought in from the laboratories of Thomas Edison. It was not used because doctor's decided things were looking so good, that there was no immediate need to locate, and remove the bullet that was still lodged in the President's body.

On Tuesday it was discovered that a small portion of the President's clothes had entered the wound when he was shot. Surgeons opened a small part of the wound to remove it, and everything seemed well afterwards.

According to doctors, the biggest concern McKinley expressed was not being allowed to smoke a cigar. The President was a cigar aficionado, and during the course of most days he would smoke ten to twenty of them.

About 8:30 Thursday evening the President suffered his first relapse. It was discovered that his bowels were not working properly, which caused a problem eliminating food in the stomach. Because of this doctors were concerned about a risk of heart failure.

Thursday afternoon McKinley's digestive organs continued to cause problems. Later that afternoon the President's pulse rose abnormally high and doctors became more concerned.

Just after 2:00 AM Friday, it was discovered that the President's heart was weakening. Doctors in attendance were sure the end was near. Digitalis and strychnia were administered, and the rest of the medical team was called back to the Milburn home.

Shortly before the President's death doctors gave him powerful heart stimulants and oxygen to restore him just enough so he could say his goodbyes to Mrs. McKinley.

President William McKinley passed away at 2:15 AM on Saturday, September 14th, 1901. He was 58 years old.

Trial and execution of Leon Czolgosz

Leon Czolgosz's trial began only nine days after the death of President McKinley. The trial opened at 10:00 AM, September 23, 1901, in the New York Supreme Court at Buffalo. Justice Thomas C. White was on the bench.

The Assistant District Attorney's statement to the jury was that the shooting was "deliberate and premeditated." Nothing was said about anarchists, conspirators, or about Emma Goldman. He was determined to focus on the facts of the shooting.

Dr. Matthew D. Mann, one of the President's physicians, testified as to the President's condition. When asked if there was anything known to medical science that could have saved the President's life, his response was, "No."

Louis Babcock, who was in charge of ceremonies at the Temple of Music on the day of the assassination, gave details about the scene of the shooting. He testified about the entrances and exits, and the position of the President. He stated that he "heard two shots. I immediately turned to the left. I saw the President standing still, and he was deathly pale. In front of him was a group of men bearing the prisoner to the floor."

Edward Rice, chairman of the committee of ceremonies, testified that he "noticed something white pushed over to the President and then two shots rang out."

According to James Quackenbush, one of the examiners who took Czolgosz's statement at the Auburn police station, Czolgosz talked about being an anarchist, and gave details of the different attempts he had made to shoot the President that week at the Exposition. According to him Leon Czolgosz confessed, "I killed President McKinley because I done my duty. I don't believe one man should have so much service and another man should have none."

At the closing of the trial Czolgosz said, "There was no one else but me. No one else told me to do it, and no one paid me to do it."

The jury deliberated for only one hour before bringing back the verdict of guilty. Justice Truman C. White pronounced the sentence,

"The sentence of the court is that in the week beginning October 28, 1901, at the place, in the manner and means prescribed by law, you suffer the punishment of death."

Leon Czolgosz stood there unmoved, as he listened to the verdict.

***

The night of September 26th, a special car was attached to the New York Central train. Leon Czolgosz arrived at Auburn State Prison at 3:10 AM on September 27, 1901.

Outside the prison gates there was a crowd of 300 angry onlookers waiting for a glimpse of Czolgosz. He was escorted from the train to the prison with a guard on either side of him. The crowd surged forward, punching and mauling Czolgosz, and sometimes the guards. A fist smacked Czolgosz in the head bringing him to the ground, and guards were forced to drag him along.

Inside the prison, the gates were thrown open, and a dozen prison guards rushed to their aid, pushing and shoving back the wild crowd. Inside the prison gates four burly guards carried Czolgosz up the steps to the warden's office. Once there he was stripped of his clothes, and given his prison uniform.

***

Warden J. Warren Mead visited Czologz in his cell at 5:30 AM on the morning of October 28th, 1901, and after rousing the prisoner from his sleep, read him his death warrant.

The walk from his cell to the electric chair was less than twenty feet. Czolgosz was wearing a gray flannel shirt open at the neck, coarse trousers, and a new pair of shoes.

Inside the execution chamber, he was strapped into the electric chair. A leather-backed sponge soaked in salt water was strapped below his knee, and a helmet was placed upon his head. The top of the helmet contained a wet sponge.

Leon Czolgosz was allowed to make his last statement: "I killed the President because he was the enemy of the good people; I did it for help of the good people, the working man of all countries."

When he was done talking a leather strap was buckled across his head. It covered his nose and eyebrows, and there was a slit for his mouth.

The word was given, and 1700 volts of electricity coursed through his body for sixty seconds. Gradually the current was reduced to 200 volts and then stopped. The body shuddered and shook in the chair.

A second jolt of 1700 volts was sent rushing into Czolgosz's body for another sixty seconds. The doctor was sent in, and after examining the body said, "Gentlemen, the prisoner is dead."

It was 7:17 AM.

The body was buried in an unmarked grave in the prison cemetery. Before burial it was soaked with acid and then covered with quick lime to thoroughly destroy any trace of the remains.

***

The Temple of Music was demolished in November of 1901 after the end of the Pan-American Exposition.

John F. Kennedy

The Presidential motorcade in Dallas, Texas

President Kennedy made a breakfast speech in Fort Worth, Texas on November 22, 1963. Shortly after that the Presidential party left Fort Worth on Air Force One. They arrived at Love Field in Dallas, Texas fifteen minutes later.

Upon landing at Love Field, the Kennedy's were met by Vice-President Johnson and his wife, who presented them with a gift of flowers. Stepping off of Air Force One they were greeted by a large crowd of onlookers, holding banners and waving at them. After shaking hands with the crowd, the President's Motorcade left Love Field at 11:40 AM that day. Riding in the limousine with President Kennedy were his wife Jacqueline Kennedy,

Texas Governor John Connally and his wife, Nellie Connally, the limousine driver, and Secret Service Agent Roy H. Kellerman, who rode in the front seat.

The President was in town for a luncheon with Dallas Civic and Business Leaders. As elections were just around the corner, the trip was supposed to help build support for Kennedy's reelection bid in 1964. Vice-President Lyndon Baines Johnson, a Texan himself, was along on the trip. He was in the fourth car of the motorcade.

In order to get maximum exposure for the President on his visit, it was decided that Kennedy would ride in an open Limousine from Love Field to Dealey Plaza. Newspapers announced the event several days beforehand, publishing the entire motorcade route so people could find a spot to see the President from. It is estimated nearly 200,000 onlookers watched the motorcade along its entire route.

The motorcade stopped several times along its route giving Kennedy time to shake hands with groups of school children, and even a group of nuns.

As the Presidential limousine reached Dealey Plaza it turned left onto Elm Street, and passed the Texas School Book Depository. Mrs. Connally testified that at this point she told Kennedy, "Mr. President, you can't say Dallas doesn't love you?"

It was just down the street from the Texas School Book Depository that the first shots rang out. Most onlookers thought it was fireworks, or one of the cars in the motorcade backfiring.

Governor John Connally testified that he turned to see the President after hearing the shot. He could not see him, so turned to look again. It was then that he was shot in the upper right section of his back.

After being shot, Connally recalled shouting, "My God. They're going to kill us all!"

Mrs. Connally testified that she "heard a noise that I didn't think of as a gunshot ... [I] turned to my right from where I thought the noise had come and looked in the back and saw the President clutch his neck with both hands. He said nothing. He just sort of slumped down in the seat.

"Then I heard a third shot and felt matter cover us." She continued on to say that she heard Mrs. Kennedy exclaim, "They have killed my husband, I have his brains in my hand."

According to Mrs. Kennedy, "my husband never made any sound. So I turned to the right. And all I remember is seeing my husband, he had this sort of quizzical look on his face, and his hand was up, it must have been his left hand. And just as I turned and looked at him, I could see a piece of his skull and I remember it was flesh colored. I remember thinking he just looked as if he had a slight headache. And I just remember seeing that. No blood or anything.

"And then he sort of did this [indicating], put his hand to his forehead and fell in my lap."

Another witness on the scene that day, James W. Altegens, an Associated Press Photographer with the Dallas Bureau, gave the following testitmony:

"I made one picture at the time I heard a noise that sounded like a firecracker ... at the time I was looking at the President, just as he was struck, it caused him to move a bit forward. There were flesh particles that flew out of his head in my direction from where I was standing."

James Tague, who was watching the motorcade nearby, was struck in the cheek by a bullet fragment.

Not too far away, was an amateur photographer, Abraham Zapruder, who captured the assassination on his 8 mm movie camera. Zapruder's film was analyzed frame by frame by the Warren Commission and subsequent investigators as they tried to piece together what happened that day. While it is not the only film taken of the assassination, it is accepted as the most complete.

Lee Harvey Oswald in his backyard, holding rifle similar to the one used to kill President Kennedy

After the shots were fired, the motorcade sped out of the area, rushing the wounded President and Governor to Parkland Memorial Hospital in Dallas. Nurse Diana Hamilton Bowron was one of the first hospital staff to arrive at the President's limousine. She testified that the "[President] was very pale, he was lying across Mrs. Kennedy's knee, and there seemed to be blood everywhere. When I went around to the other side of the car I saw the condition of his head."

Inside the hospital, doctor's concluded that the President was already dead, but made efforts to keep him alive. According to Doctor Charles Rufus Baxter, "We had an opportunity to look at his head wound then and saw that the damage was beyond hope, that is, in a word – literally the right side of his head had been blown off.

"We did not pronounce him dead but ceased our efforts, and awaited the priest and last rights before we pronounced him dead."

Another member of the hospital emergency team, Doctor Gene Coleman Akin, said "the back of the right occipital parietal portion of his head was shattered, with brain substance extruding."

Nurse Bowron helped to clean up the President's body after he was pronounced dead. According to her testimony, they stripped off his clothes and gave them to waiting secret service agents. After that, the President's body was put in a waiting coffin, and taken to Air Force One. The time was 2:00 PM, not even an hour and a half after the shooting took place.

Lyndon Baines Johnson was sworn in as President on Air Force One, just before it left Love Field in Dallas, Texas. Jacqueline Kennedy was alongside of him, still wearing her pink chiffon dress, covered with her husband's blood and brain matter.

***

Just after the shooting, Howard Brennan, reported to police that he had been sitting across the street from the Texas School

Book Depository building, and that when he looked up, he saw a man holding a rifle in one of the sixth floor windows. He also gave a description of the man that he saw.

The time was 12:45. Fifteen minutes had elapsed since Kennedy was shot.

In a matter of minutes police had all of the entrances to the Texas School Book Depository sealed off. In the sixth floor window that Brennan had pointed out to them, they found a pile of boxes where the sniper waited hidden from view. By the boxes they found a rifle, with three spent shell cases. And, from the window, as they looked out, they saw the shooter would have had a perfect view of the motorcade.

As police were searching the building, a supervisor reported that one of his employees, Lee Harvey Oswald was missing. The supervisor also told police that Oswald brought a long oblong package to work with him that morning.

Oswald's description was broadcast to authorities all over the city.

Officer J. D. Tippitt

About seventy minutes later Officer J. D. Tippitt spotted Oswald walking along the side walk in Oak Cliff, a residential neighborhood about three miles from Dealey Plaza.

According to witness Helen Maram, Tippitt began questioning Oswald from his squad car. As he was getting out of the car, Oswald shot him four times, killing Officer Tippitt.

Johnny Brewer, a shoe store manager was next to spot Oswald. According to him he saw a man lurking about outside of his building, and then he watched him sneak into the Texas Theater without paying. Brewer called the theater to let them know what he had seen, and the ticket taker there subsequently called the police.

Oswald was arrested in the theater after attempting to shoot at the police. Witnesses testified that they heard the click of his revolver, but it misfired. Oswald was said to have screamed about "police brutality" as he was dragged out of the theater. He told the police, "I don't know why you are treating me like this. The only thing I have done is carry a pistol into a movie theater."

Lee Harvey Oswald was taken into custody charged with the murder of President John F. Kennedy and Officer J. D. Tippitt. Throughout his two days of questioning Oswald denied any involvement in either crime, saying he was being set up as a "patsy."

Jack Ruby getting ready to shoot Lee Harvey Oswald

Two days later Lee Harvey Oswald was shot and killed on live TV by Jack Ruby, a Texas Night Club owner. Ruby claimed that he was so distraught by the assassination of President Kennedy that it drove him to it.

Lee Harvey Oswald

Lee Harvey Oswald was born in New Orleans, Louisiana on October 18, 1939. His father, Robert Oswald died of a heart attack, just two months before he was born.

From that point on his life was a roller coaster ride of moves and troubles with school authorities and the police. His mother moved the family to Dallas in 1945, to New York in 1951, back to New Orleans in 1954, and to Fort Worth in 1956.

Just after he turned 17, Oswald dropped out of school and enlisted in the Marines Corps on October 24, 1956. Discipline troubles dogged Lee Harvey in the Marines, as they had in is previous life. He faced court-martial charges three times, once for accidentally shooting himself in the elbow, once for fighting with a sergeant, and the final time while stationed in the Philippines, for discharging a rifle on jungle patrol without a proper reason.

He was discharged from the Marines in 1959, and within two weeks was on his way to the Soviet Union. On October 31, 1959, Lee Harvey went to the American Embassy in Moscow to renounce his American citizenship, and declared that he wanted to become a Soviet citizen.

He was given a job as a lathe operator in Minsk. Early in 1961 Oswald tired of Russia, and wrote to the American Embassy about restoring his American Citizenship. About that same time he met Maria Nikolayevna Prusakova, and married her six weeks later in March of 1961. They had a daughter, June, born on February 15, 1962.

In June of 1962 they returned to the United States, settling in the Dallas / Fort Worth area. Lee Harvey was quickly fired from a string of jobs.

In March of 1963 he purchased several weapons by mail-order under the alias "A. Hidell." One of the weapons was a .38 Smith and Wesson, and the other was a 6.5 mm Carcano rifle with a telescopic scope.

Marina Oswald later told the Warren Commission during her testimony that Lee Harvey told her he shot at right wing former General Edwin Walker. She went on to say that he buried the rifle that night to hide the evidence. The bullet was fired through his window, hit the window casing, and the General received bullet fragments in his forearm. Until the time Marina gave her testimony to the Warren Commission this case was unsolved.

After this, Lee Harvey travelled to New Orleans and Mexico, becoming involved in Cuban rights groups in both places. In October of 1963, he returned to Dallas, taking a job at the Texas School Book Depository on October 16, 1963.

During this time Marina stayed with Ruth Paine in Irving, and Oswald took a room in Dallas, going to Irving on weekends to stay with Marina. Early in November of 1963, FBI Agents visited the Paine house twice investigating Marina as a Soviet Agent.

On November 22nd, 1963, Lee Harvey Oswald was alleged to have shot President John F. Kennedy and Officer J. D. Tippitt. He was shot and killed two days later by Jack Ruby, a Texas strip club owner, said to have minor ties with the local mob.

Jack Ruby later plead that he was overcome with grief due to the Kennedy assassination, and suffered "psychomotor epilepsy" that made him unconsciously shoot and kill Lee Harvey Oswald. The jury didn't buy his reasoning, and Jack Ruby was found guilty of "murder with malice" and sentenced to die. The sentence was overturned in 1966, and a new trial was set, but Ruby died of lung cancer in 1967 before he could be retried.

The Warren Commission

The Warren Commission was created by Executive Order 11130, under the direction of President Lyndon Baines Johnson, one week after the assassination of President Kennedy.

The Commission was formed because of the public need to know what happened that day in Dallas. After the killing of Lee Harvey Oswald by Jack Ruby, there would be no trial to discover the facts behind what happened, and positively prove Lee Harvey Oswald's guilt.

President Johnson was at first reluctant to appoint a special commission to investigate the assassination, but after prodding by prominent journalists, academics, and cabinet members, he determined that a special commission was necessary to provide closure.

Members of the Warren Commission included:

- Chief Justice Earl Warren
- Senator Richard Russell
- Senator John Sherman Cooper
- Representative Gerald Ford
- Representative Hale Boggs
- Allen Dulles, former director of the Central intelligence Agency
- John McCloy, who had been a High Commissioner of Germany

Solicitor General, J. Lee Rankin acted as Chief Counsel, and had a team of attorneys working under him to take testimony and assemble the findings.

The Commission itself interviewed nearly 100 witnesses including Marina Oswald, Jacqueline Kennedy, and Governor John Connally, and his wife Nellie Connally. Over a thousand more witnesses were interviewed during the course of the investigation by the Dallas Police, the Federal Bureau of Investigation, Secret Service Agents, and special investigators. Altogether, the report contained twenty-six volumes of testimony, evidence, and findings. Nearly 98% of the material is declassified and available to the public today.

The Warren Commission delivered its findings to President Johnson on September 24, 1964.

Their conclusions were that:

- Lee Harvey Oswald was the sole assassin, and acted alone
- Three bullets were fired, at least two of which killed President Kennedy and wounded Governor Connally
- Jack Ruby acted alone in killing Lee Harvey Oswald
- Finally they stated that they "found no evidence that either Lee Harvey Oswald or Jack Ruby were part of any conspiracy, domestic or foreign…"

The FBI came to a similar conclusion in a report of their investigation given to President Johnson shortly after the assassination. Dallas Police came to the same conclusion.

***

Many conspiracy theories have been put forth since the shooting.

One such report was issued by the United States House Select Committee on Assassinations in 1978. Their conclusions were that:

- Oswald did indeed fire all of the shots that hit Connally and Kennedy.
- There were at least four shots fired. At least one was not fired by Lee Harvey Oswald.
- They concluded that "there was a high probability that two gunmen fired" shots that day.
- They did not say who was involved. They did say that it was not the CIA, Soviet Union, or organized crime. At the same time, they did not rule out the possibility of individuals from those groups acting on their own.

***

In the end, there is no solid evidence to dispute the main findings of the Warren Commission. There is no absolute proof that anyone assisted Lee Harvey Oswald in the assassination.

All of the conspiracy theories are just that: Theories.

Presidential Assassination Attempts

Andrew Jackson

Andrew Jackson is the first President to have had an attempt made on his life.

The day was January 30th, 1835.

Jackson was attending a State funeral for South Carolina Congressman William R. Davis in the House Chamber of the Capitol Building. The President was walking across the rotunda about to step out on the portico, "when a man emerged from the crowd and, placing himself before the President at a distance of eight feet from him, leveled a pistol at his breast and pulled the trigger. The cap exploded with a loud report without discharging the pistol. The man dropped the pistol upon the pavement and raised a second, which he held in his left hand under the cloak. That also misfired. The President…rushed furiously at him with uplifted cane. Before he reached him Lieutenant Gedney, of the navy, had knocked the assailant down"

This account is from Jackson's first biographer, James Parton. Other accounts have Jackson viciously attacking and clubbing his assailant with his cane, or Davy Crockett, who was also at the funeral, helping to bring down the attacker.

In any event, the attacker, Richard Lawrence, an unemployed house painter, was quickly subdued and taken to jail. At his trial it came out that Lawrence had a history of acting strangely, and blamed the President for his condition. Richard Lawrence testified that he felt the country would be better off without Jackson as President, and that things would improve with Martin Van Buren as President.

The jury deliberated for five minutes before finding Richard Lawrence not guilty by reason of insanity. He spent the rest of his life in a mental institution, dying there in 1861.

Abraham Lincoln

Many stories circulated about assassination attempts upon the life of Abraham Lincoln. Here are two of the more credible attempts made before his assassination at Ford's Theater.

Baltimore Plot. The Baltimore Plot to assassinate Abraham Lincoln was uncovered by Detective Allan Pinkerton while Lincoln was en route to Washington from Springfield for his inauguration.

Pinkerton had received reliable information that there was a plan to ambush the President's carriage between the Calvert Street Station and the Camden Street Station in Baltimore. He strongly advised the President not to make his scheduled stops in Harrisburg, Pennsylvania, or in Baltimore.

After much deliberation, Lincoln took a special train out of Harrisburg, passing through Baltimore during the night of April 22, 1861. The next morning he was already in Washington when the President's train made its scheduled stop in Baltimore. Onlookers expecting to get a look at the new President elect were disappointed to find the train contained only Mary Todd Lincoln and her family.

Lincoln took much ribbing from the press for this move, and he came to regret his decision not to stop in Baltimore.

Soldier's Home. Abraham Lincoln often rode out to the Presidential cottage at the Soldier's Home just outside of Washington. One night in August of 1864 he arrived at the cottage gate with his horse nearly out of breath. His trademark stove pipe hat was missing.

Private John Nichols who was standing guard at the gate that night heard a rifle shot, then he saw the figure of Lincoln rushing in on his horse. Lincoln told the guard his horse was spooked by the report of the gun.

Later when soldiers went to retrieve Lincoln's stove pipe hat, they found a bullet hole had pierced the crown of his hat.

Theodore Roosevelt

The attempt on Theodore Roosevelt's life came just after he had finished dinner at the Hotel Gilpatrick in Milwaukee, Wisconsin.

The day was October 14, 1912.

Roosevelt was waving his hat to the crowd when a man came up out of nowhere, and fired a shot into the former President. The bullet struck Roosevelt in the chest. At first he didn't think he was hit. But, when they checked him over in the car, there was blood on his shirt, and a bullet hole in his chest.

The shooter John Schrank, an unemployed New York saloonkeeper had been stalking Roosevelt for weeks waiting for an opportunity to take his shot. A letter was later discovered on the gunman. It said, "To the people of the United States…In a dream I saw President McKinley sit up in his coffin pointing at a man in a monk's attire in whom I recognized Theodore Roosevelt. The dead president said—'This is my murderer—avenge my death.'" And, so he dogged the former President for thousands of miles, and took his shot.

For Roosevelt's part, he was scheduled to make a campaign speech that night before thousands of people, and that he did, despite his doctors and advisors requests that he should immediately go to the hospital.

What saved his life was a fifty page speech he had, folded in two in his breast pocket, and a steel eye glass case. They slowed down the bullet just enough, so that Roosevelt wasn't severely injured. The bullet went into the chest near his right nipple, and burrowed in about three inches deep. It was never removed, and remained in the former President's body until the day he died.

That night at his speech Roosevelt told listeners, "It takes more than that to kill a Bull Moose!"

Herbert Hoover

In November of 1928 Herbert Hoover began a seven week long good will tour of Latin America. While in Argentina, Anarchist Severino Di Giovanni, attempted to blow up the railroad car that President Hoover was riding in.

Giovanni was arrested before he could plant the dynamite, but investigators discovered that he possessed copies of the President's itinerary, including trip times and dates.

The motivation for the assassination attempt was apparently to avenge the deaths of Sacco and Vanzetti.

Hoover brushed off the attempt, and continued on with his tour of Latin America.

Franklin D. Roosevelt

Franklin D. Roosevelt was shot at by a man with a stomach ache and a grudge against rich capitalists.

Shooter Giuseppe Zangara was an unemployed Italian American brick layer, some say an Italian anarchist. The shooting occurred at Bayfront Park in Miami, Florida on February 15, 1932.

Zangara was short. He was only five feet tall, and as such, was forced to stand on a wobbly metal folding chair to get a good view of President-elect Franklin D. Roosevelt. Five shots rang out that day. Five people were injured. Fortunately for Roosevelt, several people in the crowd grabbed Zangara after hearing the first shot, and threw off his aim.

Roosevelt escaped unharmed, but Chicago Mayor Anton Cermak, who was with Roosevelt that day was shot in the stomach, and soon died from his wounds.

At his trial Giuseppe Zangara told authorities, "I decide to kill him and make him suffer [Franklin D. Roosevelt] … since my stomach hurt I want to make even with capitalists by kill the President. My stomach hurt long time."

Giuseppe Zangara died in the electric chair on March 20, 1933, just over one month after the assassination attempt.

Harry Truman

On November 1, 1950 two members of the Puerto Rican Nationalists Party, Ocsar Collazo and Griselio Torresola, stormed Blair House (across the street from the White House) with the intent to kill President Harry Truman.

They approached Blair House from opposite directions and opened fire on White House Police and Secret Service agents stationed there. Over thirty rounds were fired in less than three minutes.

When it was all over three White House guards were wounded, and another one, Private Leslie Coffelt, died later that day from wounds he received in the gun battle. Torresola was shot in the head and killed. Collazzo was shot down on the steps of Blair House, but survived. He spent the next twenty-nine years in prison, until Jimmy Carter commuted his sentence in 1979.

Their plan had been to draw attention to Puerto Rico and advance the cause of Puerto Rican independence.

Truman was in the house napping, and poked his head out when the shooting ended. Less than a half hour later he left Blair House to make a scheduled speech at Arlington National Cemetery.

Gerald Ford

Gerald Ford had two attempts made on his life while he was President, both by women.

The first was by Lynette "Squeaky" Fromme, on September 5, 1975. Fromme was a member of the Charles Manson family. She approached the President while he was walking near the California Capitol Building, and pulled a .45 caliber revolver. Secret Service agent Larry Buendorf wrestled Fromme to the ground and disarmed her before she could fire off a shot.

Gerald Ford continued on to the Capitol Building to make his scheduled speech. Lynette "Squeaky" Fromme was sentenced to life in prison. The reason she gave for the attack was that she wanted to gain the attention of Charles Manson.

She was released from prison on August 14, 2009.

***

Seventeen days later Sarah Jane Moore, an accountant, attempted to shoot President Gerald Ford in San Francisco.

According to everyone, Sarah Jane Moore, was the least likely person to be an assassin. She had been married five times, had four children and was employed as an accountant. She was also involved in radical politics, and was a known FBI informer.

Two days before the assassination attempt she called authorities to warn them about her plot, and asked to be arrested. She was picked up by the FBI, who confiscated her weapon, but set her free.

The next day she purchased a .38 caliber revolver. Once again she called authorities, and asked several times to be arrested. Her plea went ignored.

On September 22, 1975 the forty-five year old Moore approached the President in San Francisco. When she was about forty feet away, she pulled her revolver and fired. The bullet barely missed Ford. She was ready to shoot again when she was tackled by Oliver Sipple, a disabled former Marine.

Sarah Jane Moore was sentenced to life in prison. She escaped briefly in 1987 by climbing over the prison fence, and was quickly recaptured. She was released from prison on December 31, 2007.

Ronald Reagan

On March 30, 1981, President Ronald Reagan had just finished giving a speech at the Washington Hilton Hotel, and was walking out to his car.

As Reagan approached the car, just a short thirty foot walk, John Hinckley opened fire with a .22 caliber revolver. He got off six shots in less than five seconds.

Secret Service agent Tim McCarthy threw himself in front of Reagan acting as a human shield for the President. He took a bullet in the abdomen.

Almost immediately after the first shot was fired Secret Service agent Jerry Parr shoved the President into the backseat of the waiting Presidential Limousine. He sped off as quickly as he could to distance Reagan from the threat. At first, neither Parr nor Reagan realized that the President was hit. As soon as he saw the blood Parr changed directions, and raced the car to George Washington Hospital.

Hinckley was subdued and taken into custody. During his trial it came out that he had a long history of mental illness. He was enamored of actress Jodie Foster, and had been stalking her for years. Hinckley though that shooting President Reagan would capture Foster's attention.

Because the whole incident was caught on film, there was no real question about his Hinckley's guilt. John Hinckley was found "not guilty by reason of insanity," and has been confined in St. Elizabeth Hospital ever since.

Along with President Reagan and Secret Service agent Tim McCarthy, two other people were shot. Presidential Secretary James Brady was shot in the head, and police officer Tom Delahanty was shot in the neck.

www.ingramcontent.com/pod-product-compliance
Lightning Source LLC
Chambersburg PA
CBHW070205100426
42743CB00013B/3054